LITTLE THINGS IN LIFE

Learn to live in the small moments;
that's when you start living.

ZUBIA HASSAN

BLUEROSE PUBLISHERS
India | U.K.

Copyright © Zubia Hassan 2023

All rights reserved by author. No part of this publication may be reproduced, stored in a retrieval system or transmitted in any form or by any means, electronic, mechanical, photocopying, recording or otherwise, without the prior permission of the author. Although every precaution has been taken to verify the accuracy of the information contained herein, the publisher assume no responsibility for any errors or omissions. No liability is assumed for damages that may result from the use of information contained within.

BlueRose Publishers takes no responsibility for any damages, losses, or liabilities that may arise from the use or misuse of the information, products, or services provided in this publication.

For permissions requests or inquiries regarding this publication, please contact:

BLUEROSE PUBLISHERS
www.BlueRoseONE.com
info@bluerosepublishers.com
+91 8882 898 898
+4407342408967

ISBN: 978-93-5819-591-0

Cover design: Tahira
Typesetting: Tanya Raj Upadhyay

First Edition: August 2023

A book which can change the perspective of your life. It will help you to change the way you look at life.

Acknowledgment

Dedicated to all those people and things who changed
the way of living life.
Who lived like an example
and
inspired others for
greatness.

THANKYOU.

Have you found someone who inspired you or
You inspired someone?

Table of Contents

1. Little Things 1
2. Solivagant 2
3. Outer Beauty is Not Everything 3
4. Why I Write? 5
5. My Place in This Story 6
6. Clouds Can Change 7
7. Medicine of Wounds 8
8. Zane 9
9. Don't Provoke Her.. 10
10. Just be Yourself 11
11. Be an Artist 12
12. The Hidden Feelings 13
13. Do What Makes You Fearless 14
14. Fightback Haters 15
15. My Life is Not a Book 17
16. The Soul and Heart 18
17. To Do Something New 19
18. Reason To Love 20
19. Boomerang of Life 21
20. A Child Inside Us.. 22
21. Don't End 23
22. Enjoy the Moment.. 24
23. Self-Happiness is Mandatory.............................. 25
24. What Will the Society Say? 26

25.	Heart Doesn't Come Down to Paper	28
26.	Don't Reveal a Secret	29
27.	Lifeless Characters	30
28.	You Never Stop Growing	32
29.	Albatross and Hodophile	33
30.	Insecurities	34
31.	Don't Stop Dreaming	35
32.	Don't Judge	36
33.	Life Under Principles	37
34.	The Story Got Over	38
35.	Sorrows Being Sad	39
36.	What Goes Up Has to Come Down Too	40
37.	Behind The Camera	41
38.	Moon Face	42
39.	Be Yourself	44
40.	Being Independent	45
41.	A Great Human Being	46
42.	All Thing Beauty	47
43.	New Beginnings	48
44.	Conflict of Heart and Mind	49
45.	Change from the Inside	50
46.	Don't React Quickly	51
47.	A Little Girl's Dream	52
48.	Mirror of Your Heart	53
49.	The Best Expression	54
50.	Forget About Me	55

51.	New Year is Here	56
52.	A Story to Tell	57
53.	Real Eyes, Realise and Real Lies	58
54.	Secrets Are Hidden	60
55.	Believe in Yourself	61
56.	Don't let Haters Get to You	62
57.	The Beauty of Flowers	63
58.	The Smile on My Face	64
59.	A Game of Lies	65
60.	It's Hard to Forget	67
61.	You Need to Thrive	68
62.	Enjoy The Moment	69
63.	Life is Abstract	70
64.	With Time it Gets Perfect	71
65.	Narcissist	72
66.	Beginning and Ending	73
67.	Time Run Like Water	74
68.	The Difference	75
69.	3 C's of Life	76
70.	Life is a Book	77
71.	Never Say Never	78
72.	Your Face, Your Eyes	79
73.	Two People	80
74.	The Weather is Beautiful	81
75.	They Leave You for A Reason	82
76.	Savouring	83

77.	Choices of Life	84
78.	Dreams and Lives	86
79.	Yildiz	87
80.	Be Tolerant	88
81.	Values	89
82.	If It Makes You Happy	90
83.	Compassion and Cooperation	91
84.	Right and Wrong	92
85.	Double Rainbow	93
86.	Travel	94
87.	Everyone's Secret	95
88.	They Don't Know	96
89.	Memories	97
90.	The Water Sleeps	98
91.	A New Day	99
92.	Inner Voice	100
93.	Pebbles in Life	101
94.	Take a Risk	102
95.	Love Yourself	103
96.	How I Feel When I Write?	104
97.	I M Possible	105
98.	How to Measure Life?	106
99.	Don't Over Expect	107
100.	Dreams to Life	109
101.	Goodness of Human	110
102.	The Last Episode	111

103. A Writer 112
104. Story Behind the Tears 113
105. Take on The World 114
106. Era of Technology 115
107. To Whatever End.. 116
108. Hurt... 117
109. A Friend.. 118
110. Do What You Can't 119

1.
Little Things

Little things in life
people usually forget to cherish
those little moments in their lives,
which makes the bigger moments.
We work so hard towards our goals that we forget
our surroundings,

Our friends and our family
And things happening around us.
Those are the little moments that matter.

The little moments in the end, add up
to bigger moments.

2.
Solivagant

Sometimes it is better
to solivagant.
It improves your mood.
You must refrain from some people and desire some peace.
Self-understanding is possible.
You are free to pursue your interest
the most.
You'll be able to keep your peace.
Tranquillity is crucial for your thinking.

3.
Outer Beauty is Not Everything

People who admire outer beauty
are obtuse.
Everyone in this world is
Beautiful,
In every way, they are beautiful.
The only thing they need is
to believe in themselves.

People should never admire the
outer beauty rather they should
admire their inner beauty.
The beauty on the inside is the
most important thing because
they make you who you are,
shows who you were,
and who you will be.

Whereas the Outer Beauty
is just the looks you have
except that it's nothing.

They will adore you for a minute and will forget it.
The only thing they will remember
is what kind of person you are.

That's your
INNER BEAUTY not
OUTER BEAUTY.

4.
Why I Write?

Everyone asks me why I write.
Does it help me?
Is there any use?

My only answer to them is
it helps me escape
from harsh reality.
The voice within me
which needs something,
could be heard through
my writing.

The voice, which has a different
perspective on life
but is been shut through people's
harsh words and humiliation.

5.
My Place in This Story

Where do I stand in this story?
It looks like I am invisible to them
or I am visible to them
when they need me
for something.

Do I have any significance in this story?
I don't think it is.
If they don't need me,
then they may remove me.

If they could,
I could create my own story,
My own world.

In my new world, where nobody
could see me, meet me,
alone with my inner peace.
Being with those people whom
I want,
who makes me happy.

6.
Clouds Can Change

Clouds never remain at
one place.
Clouds never remain at
one size.
Clouds move,
Clouds change.
If they can,
Then why don't you change
yourself?

7.
Medicine of Wounds

Time is the medicine of
wounds given in the past.
Time could heal any
wound we have.
If you give time to your
wounds, it will heal and
you won't feel the pain.
either,
the wound in your soul
or on your body.

8.
Zane

The moon and the stars.
The sun and the cotton candy sky.
The beach, the sea, and the sea shore.
The gardens filled with colourful flowers and trees around it.
The mountains covered in a white blanket of snow.
The dusk and the dawn.
The best zanes we will ever have.

9.

Don't Provoke Her

If she is quite and
not reacting to your actions.
Believe me, she is done
with your harsh words.
Don't try to push her button
because the beast inside her
is sleeping.
It's not dead.

10.
Just be Yourself

Being yourself is more important
than being somebody else in
front of others.
You could be someone else
for a limited time.
But,
One day, you have to be
the actual self.
You can't be someone for
your entire life.
You can't pretend to be someone
you are not.

It won't define
who you are.

11.
Be an Artist

You are the artist in your life.
You should be the one holding
your brush.
Don't let anyone else
paint your life.
They should not be the one
painting your life
the way they want.
You should select the colours
which you want to include
in your life.
Your life is yours
not anyone else's.
You are worth a million
things.
So is your life.

12.

The Hidden Feelings

You won't speak a word, but
your eyes will tell a million stories.
But it feels like our hearts have also learned to hide
our feelings
Or
We have forgotten how to read people's minds or
hearts.
Nowadays, it seems like people know how hide
their feelings.
We are getting good at hiding our feelings,
Or,
Wear a mask and not show what you feel.

13.

Do What Makes You Fearless

Try to do the things that
you are afraid of.
Maybe being afraid of
something stopped you from doing
what you could have done, which is
the best feeling you could
ever have.
Overcoming your fear means
trying to do the things that
would make you fight your fears.

14.
Fightback Haters

If you are in a group, then
You'll find at least one hater.

Don't be in a delusion that
The rest of them are supporting you.
They are there with you.
So, they could acknowledge you
with themselves.

There will be some who will support you during a
difficult period.
They'll be there for you when you either make it or
not.

Well, haters will aid you become
who should you be?

If you won't have at least
one Hater

then you won't be able to achieve that objective
which you have decided.
These haters will aid you in
what you believed you were incapable of.

Because you have to prove them
what you can do.
What potential do you have?

15.
My Life is Not a Book

People think that my life
is an open book.
They can judge me
the way they want.
They can read whichever
chapter they want to read.
That's their biggest mistake.
No one could read it
at their will.
You could only read those
chapter which I want
you to read.

But there are some chapters that no one could read.

16.
The Soul and Heart

A person is sick only
if his soul is sick.
Your body and soul are
one.
They are not separate.
If your soul is sick, then
it will be reflected on your
body.
If your body is sick, then
it will be reflected on your
soul.
In the end,
both our body and soul
are associated with one another.
You cannot get sick simply
by lying in bed.
Perhaps
your soul is weary
or your heart hurts.

17.
To Do Something New

If you are doing anything
for the first time.
You must~
be yourself,
feel yourself,
believe in yourself,
think as if you have
done it a million times.
This way, you wont
be nervous.

18.
Reason To Love

I was looking for a reason
to love them.
Instead, they gave me another
reason to hate them.
Ever since, I have made myself clear
that
I am not going to be the same
person as I was earlier.
To stop loving them.
The other part of my mind,
looked for another reason
to love them.
But,
they always gave me another
reason to
hate them.

19.

Boomerang of Life

I have always believed that life is a boomerang.
What goes around comes around.
It always finds a way back to you
let it be a positive or a negative thing.
You receive a reward or pay a price for your deed.
No matter how hard you try to escape from them,
they will find a way back to you because what's
written in your destiny will come back to you.

20.
A Child Inside Us

Aren't grown-up people just
little children at heart?
Every grownup has a
child
within themselves.
After countless years have passed
the kid is separated from
the flurry of activity
and coping with
the world.
Everyone seems to forget
that child,
who could just enjoy the
company of themselves.
To entertain themselves
they had unlimited options.
That little kid doesn't require
someone else to delight in
themselves.

21.
Don't End

Why do people have to end
their existence simply because
something didn't happen
as they desired.
If one thing doesn't happen,
doesn't mean you won't get
another opportunity.
You will have a million chances.
Choosing death shows how
weak-minded you are.
You ended your just
because something didn't
happen as you plan.
Just bear this in mind:
After every failure
there is success.

22.

Enjoy the Moment

Life is not only about winning
but savouring the little things.
Try to live in the moment.
This moment.
The air you breathe.
Not in the moment that has passed
or are bound to come.
Winning or losing doesn't define
your state of contentment.

23.

Self-Happiness is Mandatory

Doing what you really like
can bring so much
happiness.
But when you do things just
to please others will make them
happy.
It will not make you happy.
That will not make you
who you are.
You will just be a puppet
acting the way they want,
not the way you want.

Don't act only to appease others.
Do whatever brings you joy.

24.
What Will the Society Say?

The only factor that will
snuff down people's hopes.
Sometimes life is
"What will the society say?"
If you will consider what the
society says then you won't be able
to realise your ambitions.

Dreaming or doing things will make
the society says more,
nonetheless, we shouldn't let them
surpass ourselves.

Doing things outside of the box
something which no one
has done.

First,
you would be despised for doing that
but then,

They'll think highly of you.
They'll get along with you.

Let society say whatever
they want to say.
Their job is to say.
Your job is to be careless
about what they say.

25.
Heart Doesn't Come Down to Paper

It's better your heart doesn't
come down to paper.
Otherwise, it would take
so much time to conceal your
sensation by way of your
eyes.
Your eyes can reflect
many things.
Because a mirror it is
out of your heart.
You have to make so
much effort to conceal
your feelings.

26.
Don't Reveal a Secret

Never reveal your secret
to every friend.
I've heard that
friends also have
friends.
They may share it with
them.
It's better to keep some
secrets to yourselves.
Secrets shall be shared with
those whom you trust the
most.

27.
Lifeless Characters

The writer creates the
Story, but the actors give
life to the characters.
These actors provide a
sense that we might be
like these characters.

They leave us awestruck.
Thinking we think
we can be like them
sometimes, yet
at times, we were unable.

Lifeless characters on paper
comes to existence as a result
from them.

People begin to admire them.
People begin to believe these
characters really do exist.

Some could begin daydreaming
and picture living there.

They demonstrate that
life is perfect.
In truth, though, it doesn't
truly take place.

28.

You Never Stop Growing

Your age is the only thing
which never stops growing.
Instead, we stop growing by
living in the past.
Considering the errors
we did.
Being a part of recollections of
Individuals who never genuinely
considered us.

29.
Albatross and Hodophile

Hodophile,
the one who loves to travel.
They spend most of their
life travelling,
similar to an albatross.

Albatross spend most of
their life flying to
different continents,
different countries,
becoming a
bird of the world.

Whereas a hodophile,
who travels around the world
becomes a
man of the world.
They just have one thing
in common,
they love to travel
around the World.

30.
Insecurities

If you have any insecurities
in life,
your beauty is in it,
not the ugly you.

Attempt to accept these
insecurities as your
beauty and
not a flaw of yours.
Everyone owns a few
insecurities they possess.

If you begin embracing
them as your beauty
then you won't call
yourself or another person
ugly.

31.
Don't Stop Dreaming

I don't think so
there is anything wrong
in dreaming.
You can flee thanks to it
from the harsh reality
of life.
With the harsh truth
I mean
those things, or
truth which makes us
see the harsh
reality of life.

32.
Don't Judge

Never pass judgement on
another person's life
according to their behaviour
or stance.
We are not sure how many
wounds they have,
or how frequently they have
been hurt.
If you come across someone
who is sad,
be sure to give
them a smile.
It could brighten their day.

33.
Life Under Principles

Living your life under
Principles means
following all the regulations
you set for yourself.

Due to these principles
you may have to deprive
yourself from the person
you love.

They sometimes
deceive you,
just to keep you safe.
Living with principles is fantastic.
But, don't make it so intense that
people around you will
fear to be around you.

They are capable of lying to you
apprehensive about losing you.

34.
The Story Got Over

The story was over.
It was over in a way
that many began to cry
while clapping.
They bawled their eyes out in gratitude.
They sobbed while listening to the narrative.
After it was over
they sobbed more as a result.

35.

Sorrows Being Sad

It's just sorrow, which is
sad for no reason.
We strive to ignore the suffering.
We attempt to change our focus.
Whatever the case,
all of us have the same response:
"Everything is good;
everything is fine".
The same answer to
every question.
However broken-hearted
or how depressed we are.
The answer will remain the same.

36.
What Goes Up Has to Come Down Too

"What goes up has to
come down too".
This saying is very powerful.
Something that one should never
forget.

When a person gains power,
they start to act arrogantly.

Whenever they exhibit their
arrogance, they fail to remember
they eventually have to
vacate the post.
They might refrain from
abusing their power.
One should never stray from
their origins or core principles.

37.
Behind The Camera

Recording videos on
video cameras
to record on the phone.
We have forgotten a lot
of our life treasures
thanks to technology.
At this point in our life, everyone
is preoccupied with displaying
their virtual lives.
They make an effort that their
virtual life is as perfect as it seems.
No one knows what is going on
behind that camera.
A virtual life is not
always the reality.

38.

Moon Face

People are usually like
a moon face.
There are always two sides.
The Dark Side
which no one really sees.
It's what they are from inside.
It's the invisible side of
moon.

The Bright Side
Which only those who
see them with love.
It's what they are from outside.
It's the visible side of the
moon.

Every person consists of two parts:
One is our secret and sensitive side.
The second is,
the one that only those who

see with love will see.
Our real bright side.
Therefore, two sides.

39.

Be Yourself

Just be yourself, which is
the most important thing.
Make an effort to feel
comfortable.
You'll be able to express
yourself better.
Work as you feel.
You'll detect the distinction.
The ability to know
your feelings, and
way you communicate yourself.

40.
Being Independent

Some individuals don't want
to be reliant upon another.
They aspire to
independence.

The reasons could be
either they were left behind
or
they placed unreasonable demands on individuals.

In the end,
they discovered
that they won't seek anyone's assistance, no matter
what occurs.
They will handle every task on their own.

41.

A Great Human Being

In this world,
prior to becoming a
wonderful professional
or individual.
You should start by developing
into a wonderful person.
You won't need to please anyone
if you evolve into a great human.
You only need to
be kind and generous.
People want to work with you
just because of who you are as a
person.

42.
All Thing Beauty

Every place has its own beauty.
We each possess a certain attractiveness.
Everyone and every place have
something special.
That one thing is truly unique.
You have to find it.
Finding that particular something
will be made easier with greater self-awareness
and knowledge.
However,
when you do
make sure no one
abuses it.
Hold on to it.
Consider it your strength.

43.
New Beginnings

New beginnings need
new changes.
New changes need
a new you.
You need to
forget the past.
Forgive yourself for the
mistake done in the past.
Start a new journey with a
fresh mind.

44.
Conflict of Heart and Mind

The things we desire most are those
that we are terrified of.
Even though we may have deeply connected
desires for something or someone, sometimes our
hearts are terrified of them.
The conflict between our hearts and thoughts is now
going on and are attempting to win either one.
The most challenging struggle, though, will be to
beat any of them.
Between the two of them you struggle.

45.

Change from the Inside

People alter their appearance,
but they do not alter their
internal self.
The greater distinction is created
from how you are on the inside.
Not on the outside.

46.
Don't React Quickly

Don't react to people
quickly.
Let your patience
answer them.
If you respond quickly,
people will not offer you
any significance.
They could view you as
worthless.

47.
A Little Girl's Dream

A little girl with aspirations,
she wasn't aware that
she can't dream large for herself.
She wasn't allowed to dream.
She was expected to live her
life the way society wants
rather than her own.
She is now living her life as a
puppet, thus no matter what she
wants to accomplish, she is unable
to achieve it.
She desires to lead a significant
and unique life.
She feared doing it.
Because the society didn't
believe in her.

48.

Mirror of Your Heart

Eyes act like mirror,
Your heart's reflection.
They may reflect on something.
They can tell you everything.
Deep down inside, you don't
know yourselves.
Your heart is reflected in your
eyes. Even if you lie to someone,
the truth may eventually come to
light via your eyes.
It can show people
what is there in your heart?

49.

The Best Expression

The best expression is
a Smile.
Even a fake one does
Since no one is actually
interested in that frown.
Even your haters will be
confused with that smile.

50.
Forget About Me

You made an effort to show me
that you care, but
I found it hard to believe.
You lied to me.
You gave me tears.
You are the same as
every other person.
You've been lying to me.
You proved to me that you are one of my friends.
However, I've lost faith in you.
You made me sad.
You are the same as
every other person.
You can forget about me.
You can forget about me.

51.

New Year is Here

Another year has begun.
New promises,
New resolutions,
New plans and goals
Every year, something changes.
Occasionally, another individual
enters your life and
other times a person leaves it.
In the end, we have changed.
We are not at the exact
same place.
We are not where we
used to be.

52.
A Story to Tell

Each person has a
story to tell.
Every story is beautiful and
distinctive.
The story is ideal in
its own way.

So, grab your pen
and a notebook then
begin to write.

Turn your story into
one of the greatest books
ever written.

53.

Real Eyes, Realise and Real Lies

Real Eyes, Realise and Real Lies.
Despite how similar these three
terms seem, they have quite
different meanings.

Real Eyes-
To see people, we need eyes.
Precisely, on the inside rather
than the outside.
We have a right to know
how they are
on the inside, more than
their looks.

Realise-
We realise something,
Perhaps, something negative
that we did to someone.
Or realise what we need to do
but we failed to succeed.

We are capable of realising
anything at any time in our life.

Real Lies-
Sometimes realising the lies
takes a long time.
As someone has said:
"Lies actually spread faster
than the truth."
It's important to figure out
who is lying to you.

You need real eyes to realise
real lies.

54.
Secrets Are Hidden

Some secrets are hidden
with a lie.
Some are revealed
with the truth.
The night skies hide every secret,
but daylight reveals it.
To hide a small lie, they need
to speak another lie
which leads to a bigger lie.
When the truth comes out,
things escalate into disaster.
This gets hard to fix
the errors that we have made.

55.
Believe in Yourself

Whatever you believe
you can achieve it.
You need to
believe in yourself.
Believe in your actions.
You cannot accomplish anything
If you don't have self-confidence.
Just keep having faith
in yourself.
You won't be able to accomplish
anything in life if you quit doing it.
Never forget to believe in
yourself.

56.
Don't let Haters Get to You

If somebody hates you,
because they are not happy
with their life.
You have nothing to do with it.
They hate you just because
they are envious of your
happiness in life.
Simply never consider
what people say,
how they act.
Always attempting to put
you down,
sadden you
never, however, do that.
Just grin at them; it will be their
greatest setback and your triumph.

57.

The Beauty of Flowers

Flowers are really fun
to observe.
Ever questioned how
powerful they are.
They shed themselves in the
autumn yet emerge in the
spring as invincible.
They have improved in
both beauty and strength.
Flowers are truly evidence
that there is beauty
everywhere.

58.

The Smile on My Face

The smile, which is
on my face is
not a joyful one.
Something about this is
making me smile instead
of hiding my scowl.
However, it is getting harder to
turn because perhaps there is
something stopping me in my heart.

59.
A Game of Lies

A game of lies.
One lie she said about
being engaged to an
imaginary person.
That lie, which she has to
say to her prince.
Another lie was said by
her colleague.
They were, he said, engaged.
She was stuck in between lies.

Her lies-
She loves another man.
She doesn't like to spend
time with him.
He is not the reason why
Her face is lit up with a smile.
She doesn't love him.

His lies-

His heart doesn't break
every time he notices her ring,
or hears about her fiancé.
She is not the reason why
His face lit up with a smile.
She is not the girl he loves.

Because of all this,
when they silently communicated
with their eyes, which others
couldn't hear!
truth for the time being,
with waves of lies.
Love became the anchor and saviour.

60.
It's Hard to Forget

The things we try to forget come
to mind wherever we go.
The more we attempt to put it
out of our minds,
the more it returns.
Remembering something is
easier than forgetting it.

61.
You Need to Thrive

You can't thrive in an
environment that isn't
nourishing you.
You need an environment
where you can do
whatever you want.
Be content in all that you do.
Sometimes our surroundings
can keep us content.

62.
Enjoy The Moment

Life is what it is when
you are busy making plans.
If you are working, preparing
for something important.
You forget the moment.
This moment.
The breath you take
right now.
Because the universe
loves you,
you should let things go.

Whatever occurs,
it is for your benefit.

63.
Life is Abstract

Life is abstract.
It is not always what
they seem.
Based on one
picture we shouldn't
draw conclusions.
View the other
side of the story.
What you concluded
could just be a delusion.
Every story has two sides.

64.
With Time it Gets Perfect

Not every first time
should be perfect.
You will see changes and improvements over time.
Every little action counts
for a lot.
Everything will take time.
You won't become perfect
in a single day.
The more you do
the better it gets.

65.
Narcissist

A narcissist person.
Psychopath, sadist and
narcissist.
Narcissists are skilled at
portraying themselves as
the victims.
As they are being played,
they typically pretend
to be a victim.

But in truth,
it's them who manipulate
other people's thoughts.
They are experts at making
victims into criminals.

Their biggest weapon is the
ability to corner the victims.

66.
Beginning and Ending

Every end is a
new beginning.
Every beginning is a
new ending.
There is a beginning
and an end to
everything.
The reason being, either
finish what you have started
or don't start at all.

67.
Time Run Like Water

Don't block time.
Time will keep
flowing like water.
Water will somehow
manage whether
you like it or not.
Allow the water to run.
Life is like flowing water.
Free yourself, and
enjoy the life.

68.
The Difference

Between self-confidence
and over confidence,
there is a slight difference.
One must distinguish it.
You won't run into
any issues if
you can identify it.
You'll be able to triumph
in all contests
and trials.

69.
3 C's of Life

The 3 C's of life:
Choices, Chances, and Changes.

You must make a choice
to take a chance,
or nothing will change in your life.
Go live out the dream of
your choice.
Take the chance
change your life forever.

70.
Life is a Book

A person's life is a book.
Different stories describe
various chapters of life.
Some of them can be
readable to all but
some are closed and never
opened by anyone.
They don't want to talk
about it,
just like an old wound that
has been forgotten.

71.
Never Say Never

Never say never.
Never say you won't do
anything.
Sometimes life forces you
to perform things that
you claimed
you would never take in your
life.

72.

Your Face, Your Eyes

Your face is like an
open book.
Where I want to read
every chapter of your
life.

Your eyes have the
Depth of an ocean.
I want to drown
myself in it there.

73.
Two People

It is said that
two people are supposed
to meet.
Together,
they travel and meet at
the designated location.
Your future has everything
planned out for you,
whether you want it or not

74.

The Weather is Beautiful

The weather is astonishing.
Rain is falling, like though
someone has been cursed from
somewhere.
My face being touched by
the chilly rain.
a petrichor scent.
Little one having fun
in the rain.
Those seemingly insignificant
things may make someone smile.

75.

They Leave You for A Reason

A person doesn't leave
you just because
they want to.
There must be a reason
why they left you.

They can't help
but to go away.
You develop the ability
to carry on with your life
without them.

You will harbour a yearning
for that person but
you choose to keep
it hidden.

76.
Savouring

Savouring means taking note of the tiny things that make you joyful.
It can make you happier and help you forget those unhappy situations.
If you remember those pleasant moments instead of the sad ones.
This will help you grow spiritually.

77.
Choices of Life

You have three choices in life:
Give up,
Give in, or
Give it all you've got.

Give up, if the work
feels difficult.

Give in to the work,
completing it promptly.

Give it all you've got and
work diligently till you succeed.
If you can't, at least you might
say that, you put a lot of effort
on this particular project.
Give it all you've got
is always the best option.

The reason is that
no one would accuse you of
working without any effort.
Up to the very end,
you will work on it.

78.
Dreams and Lives

Dreams and lives.
Sometimes life is better
than dreams.
that's beautiful;
we believed too.
Because sometimes
Life awaits us
with surprises.

79.
Yildiz

Yildiz, meaning "star",
in Turkish.
The most difficult
to reach but,
the most beautiful
to look at.
The most wonderful thing
to do is to look at the stars.

80.

Be Tolerant

A man who does great things
should be tolerant of others,
even of his opponents.
Doing great things just
doesn't mean being blind;
it means they have to be
tolerant.
Be tolerant of every challenge
that comes your way.
Be vigilant with every step
you take.

81.
Values

Values change decisions.
Decisions change lives.
Adding these values to
our lives could change
our perspective.

82.
If It Makes You Happy

It doesn't have to make
sense to everyone else
if it makes you happy.
You have to perform actions
that will bring you joy.
Others won't understand
what you adore.
It is important that
you are happy and
it makes sense to you.

83.
Compassion and Cooperation

You should choose
compassion and cooperation
above rivalry.

Regardless of what you do,
be compassionate.

Whoever you work with,
be cooperative.

To achieve amazing outcomes,
work together with your
teammate and show compassion.

Be aggressive while
competing with those
you are up against,
not your teammate.

84.
Right and Wrong

What's really right for you
could be wrong for someone else.
What's wrong for you
could be right for someone else.
Just because you believe
something to be right
doesn't imply it is.
It's not always true that
something is wrong just
because you believe
it's wrong.
We do not assign
them right or wrong.
It's the behaviour,
the choice,
the needs,
of a person who determines
what is right or wrong.

85.

Double Rainbow

When you smile in the rain,
it seems though a double
rainbow arises.
They claim that just glancing
at you extends someone's lives.
Come in front of me and
add a few years to my life.
Give me a few more years
so I could fall in love,
explore the world.

86.
Travel

Travelling demonstrate
that there is a very
different world.
Different country,
different cultures,
different people and
different cuisine.

Not only you get to
explore and
eat new cuisines,
but also get to meet new people.

You can learn a lot
about a place just by
spending a week there.

87.

Everyone's Secret

A Secret.
Everyone has a secret.
Who doesn't have a secret?
They conceal it in various ways.

Some hide them with a smile.
Some hide them in their notebook.
Some hide them with siblings blood.
Some hide them in a box.

They work hard to keep their secrets hidden.
They keep their secrets private.

88.
They Don't Know

People believe they
know me quite well.
They are aware of information
about me that
I want them to know.
They are in a delusion that they
know me better than anybody else.

89.
Memories

Memories are similar to
those candy boxes.
Once opened,
you can't just take
one piece.

You can recall a lot of
beautiful stories or
moments.

You have the impression
of going back in time.

You are enjoying
those moments once more.

90.
The Water Sleeps

The water sleeps, but
an enemy doesn't.

In whatever you do,
your friend would be by
your side.
They'll watch out for you.

Your opponent would
search for these flaws.
Considering strategies
to defeat you.

To know who your
friend or opponent is,
you must be extremely
vigilant.

91.
A New Day

Every day is a new day.
New hope arises every day.
Hold on to your dream, and
Let the past go.

Start your day with a
fresh start.
Don't stress over things
that have passed.
Be concerned about the things
that are bound to occur.

The beautiful moments
that you had
planned,
dreamed, and
imagined.

92.
Inner Voice

To make an important
decision,
all you need to do is
listen to your heart.

The inner voice will be useful
to make great decisions.
Your intuition understands
which decisions are best
for you.

If your inner voice
hasn't been discovered.
Dive deep in the swamp.
There it is- the voice you
have been trying so hard
to hide.
It just needs to be heard.

93.

Pebbles in Life

Just like how the water is
full of pebbles.
Thus, there are numerous
pebbles in life.
Allow yourself to
sway with the breeze.
The pebbles will naturally
fall into position.
It'll require some time.
But once everything is
finished, it will all
look beautiful.

94.
Take a Risk

There are moments
in life where
you have to take risk
and go for it.
This is one of the
moments.

Sometimes,
decisions must be made
right away.
There isn't much time
to think of.

Be hasty in making decisions.

You must occasionally assume
a risk,
the best decisions are made
by taking a risk.

You won't progress in life
if you don't take a risk.

95.
Love Yourself

I love myself
in any form.
It is important to
be able to see the
beauty.
You must look with
your heart rather than
your eyes in order to
appreciate beauty.
If everyone begins to
view one another
from the heart.

How lovely will be
the surroundings.
You will only see the
soul.
Everyone will be
beautiful then.

96.

How I Feel When I Write?

To write poetry,
you feel the words.
The words flow
through your heart.

while writing
as the words fall
on a piece of paper,
the agony of my mind
go with it as well.

Once completed,
reading it
makes me feel so
happy and proud.

All the negative ideas
just fade away.

97.
I M Possible

Saying that something is
impossible to perform
is not acceptable.

Remember even
the word
"impossible"
is written as
I M POSSIBLE.

Everything is
possible,
until you put your
heart and soul
to the task.

98.

How to Measure Life?

Measure life by the
moments that make
you gasp for air.
Not the number of
breathes you've taken.

You always feel anxious
about everything.
Where you'll always feel
as though
you are on the edge.

You'll have anxiety and
trembling from fear
and anxiousness.
You'll experience both
life and weary.

99.
Don't Over Expect

Expectations are resentment
in the making.

If you expect anything of
someone that is beyond
their capacity.
You'll feel bad about it
and upset.

You will gradually stop
expecting things
from others.

You anticipate that you
will be the only one who
can fulfil your needs.
No other person could.

Never put too much
faith in people.

Putting too much pressure on them will make you unhappy, not them.

100.
Dreams to Life

Bringing dreams to life.
No one would be as
proud of you as you
once your dreams
came true.
When you were 15 years old,
you believed it
to be impossible.
But,
it eventually happened.
You made that dream
come true.

101.
Goodness of Human

To make people believe
in the goodness of human
you need to become the
reason of goodness.
You should serve as an example
to others
that goodness,
kindness, and
morals
still exist.
And that
they ought to treat
others nicely as well.

102.
The Last Episode

When you reach the
last episode of a show.
You started weeping.
You feel as though
a dear friend has
passed away.
A friend who
might make you
laugh,
weep, or
become enraged.
You still adore
them though.

103.
A Writer

If you write
then
you are a writer.

You don't need others
to call you a writer.
You don't have to
get your book published.
Not many books need
to be written.

If you write one
word,
that is plenty.

The most crucial
thing is that you
write, and that's what
matters.
You write,
which means you are
a fantastic writer.

104.
Story Behind the Tears

Pages filled with tears
more than words can say.
Tears may convey your
anguish better than
words ever could.
The damp piece of paper
demonstrates how much
you've sobbed.
Tears revealed the pain's
story.

105.
Take on The World

To live in your own
world,
you have to make it
yours.
The world where you
reside with the people
you love.
You must take on the
world.
Experience the world
by yourself, but
someone would be there
waiting for you at someplace.
Right where you left off.
To witness your
independence and joy.
Doing tasks without
their assistance.

106.
Era of Technology

The era of technology,
it changed us.
We were completely different
people as a result of that.
We are evolving into a new
species of humans,
who don't comprehend
human emotions, but do
grasp the emotions
expressed by
emojis and emoticons.

107.
To Whatever End

To whatever end.
An end that no one expects.
An end that everyone finds unexpected.
Abruptly ending a situation but with a backup strategy.
To return a better, stronger, and more powerful version of oneself.

108.
Hurt

You may read a wonderful
Story come to life by
hurting a writer.
Hurt a songwriter, and you'll
listen to a beautiful song
in agony.
When you harm an artist,
you will be able to see your
own works of art.
Don't hurt them; you can
end up being a contributing
factor to a masterpiece.

109.
A Friend

An old friend will never betray you.
It doesn't matter how often you two have argued or
why you don't want to be friends with them.
Due to all the shared memories and experiences,
they will never do something like this.
However, a new friend may be able to;
they only want to be your friend in order to be
near you, get close to you,
and harm you from behind.
They won't put out any effort
and will only expect stuff from you.

110.
Do What You Can't

Do what you can't!
Do the things that others have told you are impossible.
When they were unable to complete them, they were just labelled as impossible.
It does not imply that you cannot succeed.
Simply don't care and
DO IT.

www.ingramcontent.com/pod-product-compliance
Lightning Source LLC
LaVergne TN
LVHW061617070526
838199LV00078B/7321